THE LITTLE BOOK OF
MOM

Published in 2021 by OH!
An Imprint of Welbeck Non-Fiction Limited,
part of Welbeck Publishing Group.
Based in London and Sydney.
www.welbeckpublishing.com

ISBN 978-1-80069-002-8

Compiled by: Victoria Godden
Editorial: Stella Caldwell, Lisa Dyer
Project manager: Russell Porter
Design: Tony Seddon
Production: Arlene Lestrade

A CIP catalogue record for this book is available from the British Library

Printed in Italy

10 9 8 7 6 5 4

THE LITTLE BOOK OF

MOM

LITTLE WORDS OF STRENGTH, WISDOM, AND LOVE

CONTENTS

INTRODUCTION

There's a reason why one of the most common "thank you" speeches at the Oscars is a winner thanking his or her mother. With the love and support of the woman who gave us life, it feels like anything might be possible.

Anyone who is a mom knows just how tough and challenging the role can be. A mother carries her child for nine months before giving birth. Then she embarks on an endless round of feeding, bathing, teaching, and entertaining—and that's just the baby and toddler years! Motherhood can be overwhelming. It brings great responsibility and plenty of sleepless nights—and it's not even a paid job!

But of course, being a mom is also incredibly rewarding. The deep love a mother feels for her children and the heart-swelling pride she takes in them makes it all worthwhile. The special bond between a mother and child is like nothing else in the world, and it is something to be cherished.

Of course, a mother might know how to push her child's buttons. What she has to say might be difficult to hear sometimes, and she's bound to know plenty of embarrassing childhood stories! But a mother nurtures her children with unconditional love and support, helping them to grow wings and fly on their own. And even though everyone in the world has a mom, every mother-and-child relationship is something truly unique.

If you've been given this book by your pride and joy, you'll probably read its words with a knowing smile and fond memories. If you're about to become a mom, think of this as your introduction to the beautiful, truly life-shattering (in all senses of the word!) journey that you are about to embark on. Most of all, however, the following pages offer us all a moment to pause, celebrate, give thanks for, and marvel at the magical wonder of mothers.

CHAPTER
ONE

The Birth of a Mother

Becoming a mother is one of the most magical, profound, and difficult things a woman can do.

After growing and carrying your baby around for nine months, this tiny, vulnerable little bundle arrives and you suddenly have that most-revered, most-loved title of "mother."

66

Motherhood: All love begins and ends there.

99

Robert Browning

66

Life began
with waking up
and loving my
mother's face.

99

George Eliot

A mother's sacrifice
isn't giving birth.

It's nine months without
wine.

Our mother's voice is one of
the first things we ever hear, and
it's no different for birds.

It's been found that mother birds
can communicate with their
chicks while still in the egg, so
that when they do hatch, they
recognize her call.

Oxytocin, known as the love hormone, floods a mother's body during birth, reducing stress, calming her down, and helping with pain during labor.

It also hangs around after birth, too, helping a new mother feel more relaxed, well-nourished, and bonded with her baby.

In Greek mythology,
Eileithyia
was the goddess
of childbirth.

It's
estimated
that
1 in 250
pregnancies
results in
twins.

"

If pregnancy
were a book, they
would cut the last
two chapters.

"

Nora Ephron

Uplifting Birth Affirmations

Birth is the ultimate act of love.

Birth is miraculous however it happens.

Bring it on!

My baby gives me the strength to do anything.

I trust my instincts.

I fill my body and mind with good stuff.

I shake off any pressure to be perfect and simply try my best.

I am present and I am doing this.

I quiet my mind and let my body give birth.

I am strong.

66

Childbirth is
more admirable than
conquest, more amazing
than self-defense,
and as courageous as
either one.

99

Gloria Steinem

What is Hypnobirthing?

Hypnobirthing is a method of pain management that can be used during labor and birth.

It involves using a mixture of visualization, relaxation, and deep breathing techniques.

There are about

2 *billion*

mothers
in the world.

"

Our birth is but a
sleep and a forgetting.
Not in entire
forgetfulness, and
not in utter nakedness,
but trailing clouds of
glory do we come.

"

William Wordsworth

"

When you are a
mother, you are never
really alone in your
thoughts. A mother
always has to think
twice, once for herself
and once for her child.

"

Sophia Loren

Things it's OK to do when you are a new mom

Not shower for two days.

Not wash your hair for a week.

Only eat carbs.

Cry for no reason.

Forget about housework.

Forget what day/month/year it is.

Want some time away from
your baby.

Want to be with your baby
all the time.

Want your baby to go to sleep.

Want your baby to wake up
(because you miss them).

Take any help offered.

Let visitors make their
own coffee.

66

Let choice whisper in your ear and love murmur in your heart. Be ready. Here comes life.

99

Maya Angelou

66

Think of stretch marks as pregnancy service stripes.

99

Joyce Armor

"

Whatever else is
unsure in this
stinking dunghill
of a world,
a mother's love
is not.

"

James Joyce

"

There is no way to
be a perfect mother,
and a million ways
to be a good one.

"

Jill Churchill

5 top tips for new moms

Ask for help.

Build a routine.

Take care of yourself: Go for a walk, take a shower, drink a coffee!

Make healthy choices.

Remember that every stage is exactly that, a stage! And it won't last forever.

66

A baby fills
a place in your
heart that you never
knew was empty.

99

Anonymous

"

Being a mother has made my life complete.

"

Darcey Bussell

Today, women are nearly

31

when they first give birth,
whereas a generation ago the
average age was

24

The oldest woman to give birth was an Indian woman named Omkari Panwar, who delivered twins in June 2008 when she was aged **72**.

She conceived the twins—a boy and a girl—by in vitro fertilization (IVF) and gave birth via C-section.

"

Suddenly
she was here.
And I was no longer
pregnant;
I was a mother.
I never believed in
miracles before.

"

Ellen Greene

Because one of the first utterances babies make is a "ma" sound, most languages around the world have that sound as the basis for their word for "mother."

By any other name

Here are some of the different words for "mother" from around the world:

Irish: *Máthair*

Arabic: *Ahm*

German: *Mutter*

Japanese: *Okaasan* or *Haha*

Spanish: *Madre, Mama* or *Mami*

Samoan: *Tina*

Portuguese: *Mãe*

Hungarian: *Anya*

French: *Mère* or *Maman*

Swahili: *Mama*

❝

Making the decision
to have a child
is momentous. It is
to decide for ever to
have your heart go
walking around
outside your body.

❞

Elizabeth Stone

66

Ah babies. They're more than just adorable creatures on whom you can blame your farts.

99

Tina Fey

"

The two most important
days in your life are the
day you are born and the
day you find out why.

"

Mark Twain

"

I feel whole at last.

"

Meg Mathews

Mommy bloggers to boost morale

Chrissy Teigen @chrissyteigen

Kirsten Bell @momsplaining

Jennifer Anderson @kids.eat.in.color

Jessica Shyba @mamasgonecity

Laura Izumikawa @Lauraiz

Candice Brathwaite @candicebrathwaite

Liv Thorne @livesalone

Anna Whitehouse a.k.a. Mother Pukka
@mother_pukka

"

Motherhood
is the biggest
on-the-job training
scheme in the
world.

"

Erma Bombeck

66

I remember leaving the
hospital thinking,
'Wait, are they just going
to let me walk off with
him? I don't know beans
about babies. I don't have
a license to do this.'

99

Anne Tyler

66

The hand that rocks the cradle is the hand that rules the world.

99

William Ross Wallace

"

The days are long but the years are short.

"

Gretchen Rubin

Mantra

I am open
to the lessons my children
teach me.

"

Parents learn a lot from their children about coping with life.

"

Muriel Spark

66

I understood once
I held a baby in my arms,
why some people
have the need to keep
having them.

99

Spalding Gray

66

Motherhood is never being number one in your list of priorities and not minding at all.

99

Jasmine Guinness

"

Motherhood
is a wonderful
thing. What a pity
to waste it
on the children.

"

Judith Pugh

The 5 types of mother

✳

The Perfectionist Mother

The Unpredictable Mother

The Best Friend Mother

The Me First Mother

The Complete Mother

"

There's a lot more
to being a woman than
being a mother,
but there's a lot more
to being a mother than
most people suspect.

"

Roseanne Barr

"

Every mother leaves her footprints.

"

African proverb

A Mother's Love

Of all the special joys in life,

The big ones and the small,

A mother's love and tenderness

Is the greatest of them all.

Anon

66

You have to love
your children
unselfishly. That
is hard. But it is
the only way.

99

Barbara Bush

Mantra

I can do anything,
but I can't do everything.

66

I've begun to
love this creature
and to anticipate her
birth as a fresh twist
to a knot, which I
do not wish to untie.

99

Mary Wollestonecraft

According to Guinness World Records, the most children born to any woman in recorded history is

69.

The mother was a peasant from Shuya, Russia, identified only as "the wife of Feodor Vassilyev."

Birthstones

January: Garnet

February: Amethyst

March: Aquamarine

April: Diamond

May: Emerald

June: Pearl and Alexandrite

July: Ruby

August: Peridot

September: Sapphire

October: Opal and Tourmaline

November: Topaz and Citrine

December: Tanzanite, Zircon,
and Turquoise

"

Mother:
The most beautiful
word on the
lips of mankind.

"

Kahlil Gibran

CHAPTER
TWO

The Highs and Lows

Having children changes your life fundamentally, and with their arrival your view on the world alters forever.

They can light up your world and bring you joy like nothing else on Earth.

On the flip side, they can drive you up the wall and leave you questioning your sanity . . .

66

One minute you are young and cool, maybe even a little dangerous, and the next you are reading Amazon reviews for birdseed.

99

@simoncholland

Motherhood
is picking things up
off the
floor
forever.

"

Motherhood is not for
the faint-hearted.
Frogs, skinned knees,
and the insults of
teenage girls are not
meant for the wimpy.

"

Danielle Steele

Being a mom
means never needing
an alarm clock.

"

Sometimes the laughter in mothering is the recognition of the ironies and absurdities. Sometimes, though, it's just pure, unthinking delight.

"

Barbara Shapiro

66

The story of a
mother's life:
Trapped between a
scream and a hug.

99

Cathy Guisewite

THE ONLY THING KIDS WEAR OUT FASTER THAN SHOES IS PARENTS.

66

I always say
if you aren't yelling
at your kids,
you aren't spending
enough time
with them.

99

Reese Witherspoon

"

If evolution really works, how come mothers only have two hands?

"

Ed Dussault

Mantra

Your best
is good enough.

"

Being a mom has made me so tired. And so happy.

"

Tina Fey

Kids keeping you up?
Mother killer whales don't
sleep for up to two months
after giving birth
(neither do their offspring).

earned the nickname
"Mother's Ruin"
thanks to its popularity
among women in England in
the mid-eighteenth century.

Mindful mom moment

Take five while you wash your face.

Notice how the water feels when it touches your skin. How does the soap feel against your skin? What does it smell like?

For those few minutes, focus completely on the sensations of washing your face.

Sweater

*

Definition

Something you wear
when your mother gets cold.

"

The heart of a mother
is a deep abyss
at the bottom of which
you will always find
forgiveness.

"

Honoré de Balzac

"

Hugs can do great amounts of good— especially for children.

"

Princess Diana

66

A mother's arms
are made of
tenderness and
children sleep
soundly in them.

99

Victor Hugo

Mindful mom moment

Take ten mindful breaths, inhaling for a count of five and exhaling for a count of eight.

Ten breaths will feel completely different when you take them mindfully, and they will serve as a mini-meditation experience.

"

Motherhood
has a very
humanizing effect.
Everything gets
reduced
to essentials.

"

Meryl Streep

Pause, breathe, smile

"

The world is full of
women blindsided by
the unceasing demands
of motherhood, still
flabbergasted by how
a job can be terrific
and tortuous.

"

Anna Quindlen

"

You can't scare me,
I'm a mother of
teenagers!

"

Unknown

"

Mothers are all slightly insane.

"

J. D. Salinger

5 things a mom would never say

"How on earth can you see the TV sitting so far away?"

"Yeah, I used to cut class, too."

"Well, if Emma's mom says it's OK, that's good enough for me."

"I don't have a tissue with me . . . Just use your sleeve."

"Don't bother wearing a jacket, I'm sure you'll be warm enough."

"Make Mommy a drink"

(Grapefruit and Elderflower Cocktail)

Ingredients

1.5 fl oz grapefruit vodka

½ fl oz elderflower liqueur

Squeeze of fresh lemon

3 fl oz sparkling grapefruit

Ice

Instructions

Combine the vodka, elderflower liqueur, and lemon juice in a cocktail shaker and shake with the ice.

Strain and top with sparkling grapefruit.

KEEP
A
POSITIVE
MENTAL
ATTITUDE

Positive affirmation

✳

"There is
peace and love
in my home,
even in the midst
of chaos."

"

No grit, no pearl.

"

Mantra for working moms

Funny things moms say

I'm not running a
taxi service.

You treat this house like a hotel!

It's like talking to a brick wall!

Don't cry over spilled milk.

Were you born in a barn?

"

Some days I do yoga
and don't yell at my kids.
Some days I scream at
them while eating cake
over the kitchen sink.
It's called balance.

"

@katiebinghamsmith

"

Children
are like crazy,
drunken,
small people in
your house.

"

Julie Bowen

Forget dad jokes . . .

Here are some mom puns to get you through the day

Why did the baby strawberry cry?
Because his mom was in a jam!

What did the mama tomato say to the baby tomato? Catch up!

What kind of candy do astronaut moms like? Mars bars.

Why is a computer so smart?
Because it listens to its motherboard.

Silence is
golden,
unless you have
kids, then
silence
is suspicious.

6 inspirational moms in popular culture

J.K. Rowling wrote the first four *Harry Potter* books as a single mother.

Diana, Princess of Wales, mother to Princes William and Harry, famously used her status as a royal figure to support and highlight the work done by children's charities.

Marie Curie, one of the first recognized female scientists in the early 20th century, and winner of two Nobel Prizes, secured most of her achievements while raising two daughters alone.

Mary Harris Jones, known as "Mother Jones," became a union organizer and activist for child labor reform after losing her husband and four children to yellow fever in Memphis in 1867.

Michelle Obama, self-confessed mom-in-chief, made no secret of the fact that her two daughters would always be her priority even when she stepped into the role of First Lady.

Maya Angelou became a single mother to her son, Guy, at just 17. She went on to become a renowned memoirist, novelist, educator, dramatist, producer, actress, historian, filmmaker, and civil rights activist.

Recipe

Mom's iced coffee

Have kids.

Make coffee.

Forget you made coffee.

Drink it cold.

66

Children seldom
misquote you.
They more often repeat
word for word
what you shouldn't
have said.

99

Mae Maloo

66

At the end of the day, my most important job is still mom-in-chief.

99

Michelle Obama

66

Don't call me
an icon.
I'm just a mother
trying to help.

99

Princess Diana

CHAPTER
THREE

An Unbreakable Bond

There is nothing like a mother's love. It is a love so powerful that it can leave you feeling invincible!

Mothers are our teachers, our leaders, our protectors, our cheerleaders, and our champions.

"

What is learned in the cradle lasts until the grave.

"

African proverb

Life doesn't come
with a manual,
it comes
with a

mother

66

A mother's love for
her child is like nothing
else in the world.
It knows no law, no pity.
It dares all things and
crushes down remorselessly
all that stands in its path.

99

Agatha Christie

In 2014, you might have heard the heart-warming story of a cat unexpectedly mothering a clutch of ducklings.

The cat had recently given birth and when the ducklings hatched soon after, instead of seeing them as prey, she incorporated the fluffy newcomers into her own brood.

8 best qualities of a mother

Patience

Strength

Empathy

Respect

Authority

Support

Love

Kindness

66

The best
place to cry is on a
mother's arms.

99

Jodi Picoult

66

She discovered with
great delight that one does not
love one's children just because
they are one's children, but
because of the friendship formed
while raising them.

99

Gabriel García Márquez

"

Mother love
is the fuel that enables
a normal
human being to do
the impossible.

"

Marion C. Garretty

"

There is only one pretty child in the world, and every mother has it.

"

Chinese proverb

66

Sooner or later
we all quote
our mothers.

99

Bern Williams

66

All I know is that I carried you for nine months. I fed you, I clothed you, I paid for your college education. Friending me on Facebook seems like a small thing to ask in return.

99

Jodi Picoult

66

Giving advice comes
naturally to mothers.
Advice is in the genes
along with blue eyes
and red hair.

99

Lois Wyse

"

My mother taught me to walk proud and tall 'as if the world was mine.'

"

Sophia Loren

❝

A mother is the truest friend we have, when trials heavy and sudden, fall upon us . . . [she will] endeavor by her kind precepts and counsels to dissipate the clouds of darkness, and cause peace to return to our hearts.

❞

Washington Irving

Mom-to-mom advice

If you do what you've always done, you'll get what you've always gotten.

10 "Momisms"
(classic mom phrases)

Wear a coat!

One day you'll thank me.

I'm going to count to three.

I said, "No!"

I'm not going to repeat myself.

Ask your father.

You will always be my baby.

I will always love you, no matter what.

Because I said so.

Go play outside, it's a beautiful day!

66

Alone a child runs fast, with a mother slow, but together they go far.

99

African proverb

66

All mothers are working mothers.

99

Unknown

"

I want my children
to have all the things
I couldn't afford.
Then I want to move in
with them.

"

Phyllis Diller

66

There were times
when I didn't have a lot
of friends. But my mom
was always my friend.
Always.

99

Taylor Swift

"

The older I get the more of my mother I see in myself.

"

Nancy Friday

"

Yes, Mother.
I can see you are flawed.
You have not hidden it.
That is your
greatest gift to me.

"

Alice Walker

66

I remember my mother's prayers and they have always followed me. They have clung to me all my life.

99

Abraham Lincoln

66

The strength of a mother is in the ears and on the lips.

99

Mali proverb

It's spicy!

Universal Mom Code for

"I don't want to share."

66

God could not
be everywhere
so he
created mothers.

99

Proverb

"

To describe my
mother would be to
write about
a hurricane in its
perfect power.

"

Maya Angelou

66

I love being a mother . . .
I am more aware.
I feel things on a deeper
level. I have a kind of
understanding about my
body, about being
a woman.

99

Shelley Long

"

Motherhood is mind-blowing.

"

Britney Spears

66

Once you become
a mother, your heart is
no longer yours . . .
My daughter is the
greatest thing I'll ever do
in my life.

99

Kim Basinger

"

My daughter thinks I'm nosy. At least that's what she says in her diary.

"

Sally Poplin

66

Oh, my son's my son
till he gets him a wife.
But my daughter's my
daughter all her life.

99

Dinah Maria Mulock Craik

"

There is a point when
you aren't as much mom
and daughter as you
are adults and friends.
It doesn't happen for
everyone—but it did
for Mom and me.

"

Jamie Lee Curtis

66

A mother is a daughter's best friend.

99

Unknown

"

A man loves his sweetheart the most, his wife the best, but his mother the longest.

"

Irish proverb

66

I got it from
my mama.

99

Will.i.am

7 types of mother-daughter relationships

The Sisters

The Role Reversal

The Strangers

The Mismatch

The Best Friends

The Ambitious and the Executor

The Authoritarian and
the Submissive

66

My mother is a
walking miracle.

99

Leonardo DiCaprio

66

All women become like their mothers. That is their tragedy. No man does. That's his.

99

Oscar Wilde

66

Sons are the anchors of
a mother's life.

99

Sophocles

145

66

All I am I owe to my mother.

99

George Washington

66

Men are what their mothers made them.

99

Ralph Waldo Emerson

"

My mother had a great deal of trouble with me, but I think she enjoyed it.

"

Mark Twain

66

My mother never gave up on me. I messed up in school so much they were sending me home, but my mother sent me right back.

99

Denzel Washington

"

Who's a boy
gonna talk to if not
his mother?

"

Donald E. Westlake

66

Your most valuable
parenting skill is
learning to manage
yourself first.

99

Dr. Laura Markham

5 amazing things moms do and rarely get thanked for

Wipe bottoms, noses, and anything else without blinking an eye!

Survive on little sleep.

Know where everything is.

Clean up constantly.

Pack a bag for a day out (water, snacks, wipes, change of clothes, toys, diapers).

66

Everything I am
or ever hope to be,
I owe to
my angel mother.

99

Abraham Lincoln

10 iconic mothers in literature

Molly Weasley
(*Harry Potter*, J.K. Rowling)

Marmee
(*Little Women*, Louisa May Alcott)

Mother (*The Railway Children*,
Edith Nesbit)

Moominmamma
(*The Moomins*, Tove Jansson)

Ma
(*Room*, Emma Donoghue)

Grandmamma
(*The Witches*, Roald Dahl)

Catelyn Stark (*Game of Thrones*,
George R. R. Martin)

Mrs. Bennet (*Pride and
Prejudice*, Jane Austen)

Marilla Cuthbert (*Anne of Green
Gables*, L. M. Montgomery)

Mrs. Murry (*A Wrinkle in Time*,
Madeleine L'Engle)

66

Who ran to help me
when I fell,
And would some pretty
story tell,
Or kiss the place to
make it well?
My mother.

99

Ann Taylor

One of the most interesting mothers in literary history is Grendel's mother from *Beowulf*. She attacks Beowulf's army to avenge the death of her son, the monster Grendel.

66

I love my mother
for all the times
she said absolutely
nothing.

99

Erma Bombeck

66

My mother was
the one constant in my life.

99

Barack Obama

66

As long as a woman
can look ten years
younger than
her daughter, she is
perfectly satisfied.

99

Oscar Wilde

66

That dear octopus
from whose
tentacles
we never
quite escape,
nor in our
innermost
hearts
never
quite wish to.

99

Dodie Smith

CHAPTER
FOUR

Mother Nature

Mother's Day is a wonderful time to pause and celebrate our beautiful moms!

The accomplishments of human mothers are amazing, and maternal instinct is one of nature's most uncompromising laws.

Sunshine

My mother, my friend so dear,

Throughout my life you're
always near.

A tender smile to guide my way,

You're the sunshine to light
my day.

Anon

66

Of all the rights
of women,
the greatest is to
be a mother.

99

Lyn Yutang

In the UK and Ireland, Mothering Sunday, or Mother's Day, always falls on the fourth Sunday in Lent, and has been celebrated since the Middle Ages.

Mother's Day
is celebrated on the
second Sunday
in May in the
USA, Canada,
New Zealand, and
Australia.

Top 10 movies for Mother's Day

The Parent Trap (1961 or 1998)

Mamma Mia! (2008)

Steel Magnolias (1989)

Freaky Friday (1976 or 2003)

Terms of Endearment (1983)

Stepmom (1998)

Postcards from the Edge (1990)

Lion (2016)

The Sound of Music (1965)

Lady Bird (2017)

Mother's Day
is celebrated in
46 countries
around the world.

When, in 1914,
President Woodrow Wilson made
Mother's Day an official holiday,
the resolution declared:

"The American mother is doing so
much for the home, for moral uplift,
and religion, hence so much for
good government and humanity."

Americans
spend an estimated
$2.56 billion
on flowers
for Mother's Day.

Pink carnations are the flowers that represent a mother's love.

"

Who built the
drum knows best
what's inside.

"

Burundi proverb

In Norway, Mother's Day is always on the second Sunday in February, Russia celebrates it on the last Sunday in November, and in Indonesia, it's celebrated on 22 December.

66

A mother is a mother still, the holiest thing alive.

99

Samuel Taylor Coleridge

66

Biology is the least of what makes someone a mother.

99

Oprah Winfrey

The mother who
gives birth to
the largest baby on Earth is
a mother elephant.

After enduring
22 MONTHS
of pregnancy,
she will give birth to a
200LB
calf.

Female emperor penguins
leave their egg with
the male to go out in search
of food.

They travel up to

50 MILES

to reach the ocean and fish,
returning to regurgitate
the food for the
newly hatched chicks.

Mothers
with
teenagers
know
why animals
eat their
young.

A record-breaking feat of mothering endurance was reported in July 2014 when scientists observed a female deep-sea octopus brooding her eggs for four and a half years.

During the first two years
of an orangutan's life,
the young rely entirely on their
mothers for both food and
transportation.

The moms stay with
their young for

6-7 YEARS.

In addition, female orangutans
are known to visit their
mothers until they're

15 or **16.**

Elephants live
in a matriarchal society.
Females in the herd
will teach a newborn calf
how to nurse.

"

Sometimes
the strength of
motherhood is
greater than
natural laws.

"

Barbara Kingsolver

66

Children reinvent the world for you.

99

Susan Sarandon

Shortest Mother's Day poem

*

You're my mother,
I would have no other!

Forest Houtenschil

In 1920, the government of France began awarding medals to mothers of large families in gratitude for their help in rebuilding the population after so many lives were lost in World War I.

Each October, Hindus honor Durga, the goddess of mothers, during the ten-day festival known as Durga Puja.

Mother's Day is one of the biggest days for flower sales in the USA.

It is also the day on which the most long-distance phone calls are made.

Around
113 million
cards are sent on
Mother's Day
in the USA.

In Thailand, Mother's Day is celebrated on 12 August, the birthday of Queen Sirikit.

66

I am sure if the
mothers of various
nations could meet,
there would be no
more wars.

99

E. M. Forster

"

It will be gone
before you know it.
The fingerprints
on the wall appear
higher and higher.
Then suddenly
they disappear.

"

Dorothy Evslin